SNAILS

For a free color catalog describing Gareth Stevens' list of high-quality books and multimedia programs, call 1-800-542-2595 (USA) or 1-800-461-9120 (Canada). Gareth Stevens Publishing's Fax: (414) 225-0377.
See our catalog, too, on the World Wide Web: http://gsinc.com

Library of Congress Cataloging-in-Publication Data

Fisher, Enid.
    Snails / by Enid Fisher ; illustrated by Tony Gibbons.
      p. cm. -- (The New creepy crawly collection)
    Includes bibliographical references (p. 24) and index.
    Summary: Describes the physical characteristics, behavior, and natural environment of different types of snails.
    ISBN 0-8368-1581-5 (lib. bdg.)
    1. Snails--Juvenile literature. [1. Snails.] I. Gibbons, Tony, ill. II. Title. III. Series.
QL430.4.F57 1996
594'.3--dc20   95-54171

This North American edition first published in 1996 by
Gareth Stevens Publishing
1555 North RiverCenter Drive, Suite 201
Milwaukee, Wisconsin 53212 USA

This U.S. edition © 1996 by Gareth Stevens, Inc. Created with original © 1995 by Quartz Editorial Services, 112 Station Road, Edgware HA8 7AQ U.K.

Additional illustrations by Clare Heronneau.

Consultant: Matthew Robertson, Senior Keeper, Bristol Zoo, Bristol, England.

Printed in Mexico

1 2 3 4 5 6 7 8 9 99 98 97 96

THE NEW
CREEPY CRAWLY
COLLECTION

SNAILS

by Enid Fisher
Illustrated by Tony Gibbons

Gareth Stevens Publishing
MILWAUKEE

Contents

Getting to know snails

Holes in the lettuce again! Snails have been coming out at night, while you're asleep, and feasting at midnight in the vegetable patch.

These slow animals are known as *mollusks*. They have no bones, live in shells, and were among the first creatures on Earth. Fossils have even been found that are 400 million years old.

Snails belong to a group of mollusks called *gastropods*. They are related to sea creatures such as clams, limpets, and octopuses. Most types of snails, in fact, live in water.

But what is a snail's life like? Do they haul a heavy shell around all the time? How do they mate?

In the pages that follow, let's go on a journey among dead leaves and along riverbeds to find out. Join us on the snail trail!

Backpack

It's easy to recognize a snail because it always has a shell. If you see a little creature that doesn't have a shell, but looks like the inside of a snail, it's probably a slug.

Snail shells come in all shapes and sizes. They can be round or pointed, smooth or knobby. Many are a drab brown color, with a few spots and marks. Others may have bright red and yellow lines.

A snail doesn't have a face like yours or many other animals. It has four spikes, or tentacles, at the front end — two small and two large. Can you see a tiny eye at the end of each of the long tentacles?

A snail can't see much, but it can tell if it's light or dark. The two small tentacles can smell, taste, and feel, helping the snail find its next meal.

A snail's tentacles lie behind its mouth. Its unique tongue is called a *radula* and has up to 25,000 "teeth," or sharp edges. The snail patiently grinds its way through food. You can even hear it munching through crisp lettuce!

An opening in the snail's right side leads into a space called the *mantle cavity*, which functions as a lung to help the snail breathe. The *mantle* lines the inside of the shell, which helps protect the snail's body.

A snail's shell has growth lines, so you can tell how old it is by the number of lines. The shell is made of a strong, chalky material that keeps out heat, cold, and unwanted strangers — just like *your* house does.

7

At a snail's

"If you think I'm slow, just *you* try carrying *your* house around with you all the time and see how fast *you* can move!

"I don't have any legs, but the whole underside of my body, or belly, is my 'foot.' My family name, *gastropod*, actually means 'bellyfoot.'

"Apart from hauling my shell around, I'm also slow because moving along on my belly takes great effort.

"I have muscles all the way along my foot that ripple from my tail to my head. Rippling my muscles once doesn't get me very far, though. I have to do it over and over again, and it's very tiring. But I do move gracefully.

"I can make life easier if I make some mucus, which oozes out of small holes along the side of my body, and pump it under me. This helps me slide along the ground. You could say I almost swim along on dry land.

pace

"This mucus that I make is sticky, too, so I can climb walls and windows without falling off. What I can't do is glide around without anybody noticing. My mucus is a shiny, silvery color. So when you see slimy trails all over your garden path, you'll know a snail has been around."

Water

Over three-quarters of all snail species live in water all the time. They live in ponds, rock pools, babbling brooks, mighty rivers, or deep, blue lakes — anywhere in the world. Snails like damp places in which to live.

Most snails are air-breathers and come up for gulps. But some snails stay under water all the time and even have gills to take oxygen out of the water. They often lurk at the bottom of the water, out of the way, so it may be hard to find them.

lovers

Other snails are a lot bolder. They live just underneath the surface of the water, perhaps floating upside-down, like the snail shown in the illustration below. They feed on the slimy green blanket of algae that often covers the surface of ponds.

Freshwater snails don't mind how cold the water gets, as long as it doesn't freeze. In sunny weather, they hide under rocks and in deep crevices to escape the heat. Some snails, such as the marsh snail, are even happy living in the water of stagnant ponds.

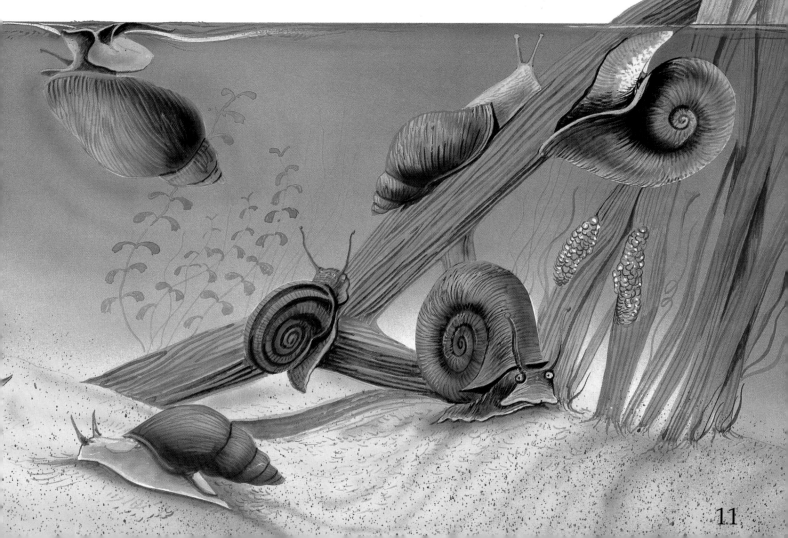

Single-sex

Like humans, most types of living beings are divided into males and females. But snails are both male and female rolled into one body. This type of creature is called a *hermaphrodite*.

Snails still cuddle up to each other as part of the mating process, just like many other creatures. So when one snail wants to mate with another snail, it will glide up to a likely partner.

It does this at its usual slow pace; soon, they both begin to perform a kind of dance. They are really just circling around to see if they like the look of each other.

They then try to get to know each other better by stroking each other's tentacles.

Eventually, the snails lie with their right sides together. This is the closest they can get to one another with those bulky shells on their backs.

creatures

The male and female parts of the snail's body are just behind its head. When two snails lie closely together, they can each be *both* the female and male.

This is in keeping with their hermaphrodite nature. And, because snails do *nothing* quickly, mating can take several hours. After mating, the snails go their separate ways. In a few weeks, both snails will be ready to lay eggs. Before long, a new generation of snails hatches.

If you eat at a restaurant in France or any restaurant that serves French food, you will almost always see the dish *escargots* on the menu. This is the French word for snails.

The type of snail most likely to end up on a dinner plate is the so-called Roman snail, with a shell over 2 inches (5 centimeters) high. This snail is easily caught and then fed fresh food to clean out its insides. This way, people won't be poisoned by something the snail might have eaten before it was caught.

Garden snails are also bred for eating by humans,

but you must never eat them straight from the garden! The decayed food they eat will still be inside them, and this could make you very sick.

14

menu

The kinds of snails humans eat are boiled in their shells. Eight or nine are usually served on a plate, with a hot garlic butter sauce. Only the soft body is eaten. A special fork is used to pull the snail out of its shell.

People who enjoy shellfish, such as oysters, clams, and mussels, also sometimes find sea snails — whelks, particularly — very tasty, too. For others, the very thought of eating a snail might be disgusting! In fact, the man in the background of this picture does not seem to like the idea.

15

Closing up shop

Imagine you're a snail and you've been up all night, munching your way through an old cabbage leaf. The sun begins to peep over the horizon. Oh, no, another hot day!

You like it best when the weather is damp, but not raining. You don't really like getting wet. But dry, sunny, summer days will be the death of you if you don't get indoors quickly.

If you've been a clever snail, you'll have slithered to someplace shady, like the inside of a flower pot or the side of a leafy tree.

If not, you'll just have to clamp down the open end of your shell hard on the ground and hope for the best.

One or two of your cousins have a front "door," called an *operculum*, to slam against that awful heat.

Others produce a sticky mucus layer, or *epiphragm*, that covers the hole in their shells.

16

You also do this in the winter because you don't like the cold, either. Besides, in winter there's hardly anything to eat. You need to find a safe place to rest.

It's important to stay hidden. You look for an ideal spot, like a crack in a wall or under a stone or log.

You'll stay out of sight there for weeks during the winter, but hungry birds will be around. They could be desperate for a good meal, and might like a snail for their dinner.

You'll know when it's time to start moving and feeding after the winter's hibernation. The weather will feel warmer, and you can now stretch yourself out. Then you can look for your first great feast of the year — a few fresh lettuce leaves, maybe!

Record

The smallest snail known, tiny *Punctum pygmeum*, would fit on the head of a pin with room to spare. But the largest land snail, the great African snail, *Achitina*, has a shell at least 6 inches (15 cm) tall.

According to the *Guinness Book of Records*, one snail from Sierra Leone in western Africa was given the humorous pet name Gee-Geronimo. It grew 15 inches (39 cm) from head to tail and weighed a hefty 2 pounds (900 grams). In Britain, the edible Roman snail has been known to have a shell 4 inches (10 cm) tall.

The fastest garden snail and the world record-holder for speed is one called Archie, owned by a young British boy named Carl Bramham.

breakers

In July, 1995, Archie covered a 13-inch (33-cm) course in two minutes. At this speed, Archie would take just over a week to crawl 1 mile (1.6 kilometers).

There is also a world record for eating the most snails. A man from La Plata, Maryland, swallowed 350 snails in 8 minutes, 29 seconds. He probably got a stomach ache!

You might like to organize a snail race among your friends. Each of you should have one snail. Mark out a course on a large sheet of paper, with a starting line and a finish line, like the one in this illustration.

Place all the snails behind the starting line. Ready, set, go! The first snail past the finish line wins.

Meet the

There are at least sixty thousand different species in the gastropod family. But you won't find them all in your garden because most species live in or near the sea.

▼ A whelk, like the one *below*, is a sea snail that eats shellfish. It grabs mussels with its foot and opens them with its shell. The fearsome dog whelk even uses its tongue, or radula, like a drill to bore a hole in the shell of its next dinner.

▲ Limpets, *above*, look like circular pyramids. They cling to rocks and stay put until high tide eventually covers them. Then they eat algae growing on the rock. You may have seen limpets on the beach at low tide. Sometimes you can even spot spaces among the algae where limpets had their last meal.

gastropods

Slugs are also gastropods. They are even peskier in the garden than snails, eating all kinds of plants and flowers. Some are even meat-eaters. They burrow underground to catch earthworms, and then suck them up just as *you* might eat a strand of spaghetti.

Snails also have relatives that live under the water, or that float.
▲ The sea butterfly (*above*) fans out parts of its mantle to keep it afloat.
▼ The bubble raft snail (*below*) traps bubbles into a trail of mucus. It clings to this "float" and feeds on passing creatures.

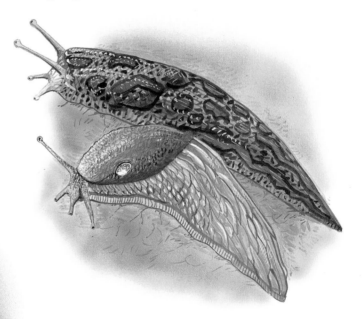

▲ Most slugs look like snails without the large shell. But many have just a tiny shell on their back, or even inside their bodies, just under the mantle.

Did you know?

▼ *Are there any snails that are dangerous or poisonous?*
The cone snail fires "teeth" like arrows that contain deadly poison at passing fish. The poison is even strong enough to kill a human. The glaucous sea snail becomes poisonous by eating the stings of the porpita jellyfish and storing them in tentacles on its back to use against predators.

Can a snail survive without its shell?
A snail's shell is part of its body for its entire life. It cannot shed it or grow a new one. Some snails can repair damage to the inside of the shell. Once the outer casing is broken, however, the snail dies.

What is a snail shell made of?
A snail's shell has three layers. The part you can see is a horny layer, like the hard bony shell found on some insects. This covers a thin, chalky layer. Right inside the shell is the *nacre*, or shiny mother-of-pearl layer.

▶ *Can you keep a snail as a pet?*
Snails are wild animals, but they can be kept as pets. A large jar or box with air holes in the lid can be used for their home. Make them a bed of soil and leaves. You can feed them lettuce leaves and fruit, and also cuttlefish bones to build healthy shells.

Are snails useful creatures?

Many types feed on algae, the green slime that often chokes the surface of ponds and fish tanks. Without snails helping to clear the water's surface, fish and other water creatures could easily become starved of the oxygen they need.

▼ Do snails have enemies?

Some species of birds swoop on land snails and carry them high into the air. They then drop the snails on a chosen stone, smashing the shells and eating the soft insides. Some birds can even crack snail shells in their beaks. Other animals, such as frogs and toads, will also eat snails if they can crack the shells. Clams eat many types of sea snails. Large snails may even crack the weaker shells of smaller snails and eat them.

▲ How are snails born?

About two weeks after mating, both snails lay up to forty eggs in the ground. These eggs are covered with soil until they hatch. The baby snails then eat their eggshells. They go through a larval stage *before* hatching, since a snail larva cannot survive outside the egg.

▼ Are snails intelligent?

Snails do not have a brain like ours. Instead, they have a system of nerves that warns the snail of danger and helps it know which way is up.

Glossary

algae — plants that grow in water and lack true roots, stems, and leaves.

fossils — the remains or traces of an animal or plant embedded in rock.

gills — breathing organs.

hermaphrodite — an animal or plant having both male and female reproductive organs.

hibernation — a state of inactivity during the winter, in which body functions of some animals slow down.

mantle — protective lining of a snail's shell.

mollusks — animals with soft, unsegmented bodies in a hard outer shell.

mucus — a slippery substance produced by the body of an animal.

operculum — the hard plate on the back surface of a snail's foot that closes the shell.

radula — in mollusks, a flexible, tongue-like organ with rows of horny teeth on the surface.

slug — a snail-like land animal without a hard shell.

Books and Videos

Interesting Invertebrates: A Look at Some Animals Without Backbones. Elaine Landau (Franklin Watts)

Mollusks. Joy Richardson (Franklin Watts)

No Bones: A Key to Bugs & Slugs, Worms & Ticks, Spiders & Centipedes, & Other Creepy Crawlies. Elizabeth Shepherd (Macmillan)

Snails and Slugs. Chris Henwood (Franklin Watts)

The Life Story of the Snail. (Encyclopedia Britannica Educational Corporation video)

Mollusks, Snails, Mussels, Octopuses, and their Relatives. (Encyclopedia Britannica Educational Corporation video)

Index